LIFE'S WAY UNTIL

POEMS ON FAITH HOPE SALVATION

ALPHONSO CRAWFORD

Copyright © by Alphonso Crawford

All rights reserved. No part of this book may be reproduced or transmitted in any form or by any means without written permission of the author.

ISBN 978-0-935379-15-0

Published by New Life Educational Services
P.O. BOX 96
Oak Lawn, Illinois 60454

Printed in the U.S.A.

FOREWORD

How gratifying it is to know that even though some consider poetry a lost or dying art in parts of the Western World, someone yet enshrines their powerful means of expression within his heart. I am adverting to Dr. Alphonso Crawford, who within this book gives an admirable account of himself. Admirable to me are the spirituality of the individually and the spiritual aura which surrounds the whole work.

His literary talents betokens a strong sense of dedication to God. A fact which prompts him to pen boldly the various facets which make up the radiant diamond of God's love for humankind. Prayer, faith in God, salvation, hope—all of these and numerous other attributes are poetically and powerfully dealt with by brother Crawford. Thus it is with deep respect and gladness that I recommend his writings to saved and unsaved alike.

Humbly submitted:
Rev. Donald E. Henton
Monument Of Faith
Chicago, Illinois

In these poems you have opened your soul to us and the result is remarkable. I trust others will be blessed and encouraged as they discover through your pen the reality of God's redeeming love and grace. May God bless you as you continue to serve the body of Christ.

Melvin E. Banks
Urban Ministries Inc.
Chicago, Illinois

In a world of dissonance where strident sounds are dominant it is rare but nevertheless pleasing to read words of wisdom reposed in inspirational thought—thank you for the charge.

Dr. Nathaniel Jarret
National Director of Youth Ministry
A.M.E. Zion Church

A significant work for our times. These poems project the truth very passionately with a spiritual alacrity that is so stimulating.

Rev. Tracy Allen
Soul Set Free Telecast

TABLE OF CONTENTS

LIFE'S WAY UNTIL	1
CRY TO GOD	3
FOUNTAIN OF LIFE	5
WHY	7
THIS IS THE WAY	8
PROJECT THY TRUTH	10
REFLECTIONS OF TAINTED SIN	11
YOUTH FOR CHRIST	12
DOES CHRIST UNDERSTAND	13
DEATH	14
FAITH TEMPLE	15
GOD IS A STABILIZER	17
TRY IT GOD'S WAY	18
HUNGRY AND THIRSTY	19
THE FATHER'S WILL	21
WORLDLY SORROW	22
THE MASTER CARES	23
SPIRITUAL EXERCISES	25
WHATS THE USE	26
DIABOLICAL MIND	27
LOVE AND HATE	28
MYSTERIOUS WAYS	29
KINGDOM OF HEAVEN	30
OVERCOME THE WORLD	31
PRAY FOR ME	32
PRAYER OF FAITH	34

FATHER HOW LONG	35
TURN US AGAIN	37
REVIVE ME	39
FORTHCOMING BOOKS BY ALPHONSO CRAWFORD:	41
FORTHCOMING BOOKS BY ELEANOR CRAWFORD:	43
FORTHCOMING BOOKS BY BYRON CRAWFORD:	44
SIGN UP AND BE NOTIFIED FOR SEMINARS/WORKSHOPS/CONFERENCES	45
SEMINARS/WORKSHOPS/CONFERENCES	46
ABOUT THE AUTHOR	48

LIFE'S WAY UNTIL

Life is very concise
Full of troubles and woes,
Forces invariably oppose you
These assiduous foes.

It appears and vanishes away
Life is a vapor.
Struggling all your life as a hireling
On some strenuous labor.

Tumultuous resultant problems
That are so complex.
Poignantly multi-dimensioned
Precipitates stress.

Suffering in this dire state of agony
With affliction and oppression,
Melancholly relatively because of
This endless regression.

No hope for tomorrow
This is the edge of night.
Is it possible somehow
To transcend this blight.

In the midst of this vast darkness
Hear the preacher's voice,
Run swiftly to the altar
Become God's choice.

Life's course will then be altered
You will see the sunshine,
And testify like many others
I am so glad that He is mine.

Life is more beautiful
Than I ever thought,
Salvation for all
Redemption blood bought.

Life is very complete
Joy radiating from the heart,
In this blessed plan
Everyone can have a part.

Happiness, righteousness, peace
No more strife,
His loving-kindness
Is better than life.

CRY TO GOD

God's ears are open
To the feeble cries.
He will strengthen you
For the cloudy skies.

You may be in dire need of Him
You may cry until you faint.
Cry with anchored hope
The weakest is the strongest saint.

Cry to Him in faith
To Him draw nigh,
He gives power to the faint
Jehovah the most High.

He will not tarry
In haste, He will move, from above.
Though circumstances produce a goliath
He will preserve you in His love.

Save me, Oh God
My problems have almost crushed me,
Help me now, Oh Lord
Hearken to my plea.

Cry to Him
He is a rock in a weary land.
Pour out your heart
He will lift you out of sinking sand.

I would have died
But my life clinged to my desire
Finally God touched my heart with joy
Liken to Holy Ghost scorching fire.

I have not been forsaken at all
But rather in His right hand upheld.
He holds my tomorrow
Now all is well.

Don't hold back the tears
Those that weep,
Go from strength to strength
All of them will God keep.

FOUNTAIN OF LIFE

Rivers of living water...stream on
Stream through the mount—
Flow freely,
Through the fount.

Source of divine energy
Stream on...stream on,
Spring of vitality
Stream on...stream on,
Spurt spiritual alacrity
Stream on...stream on

Fill the wells of salvation...rolldown
From the mount,
Spout up
Through the fount.

Rivers of living water...stream on,
Stream through the mount,
Flow freely
Through the fount.

Grant every believer, salvation.
Grant every partaker—justification.
Grant every drinker—regeneration.

Fountain of life,
Flood now...over my soul.
Now make me
Truly whole.

Fountain of life...
Let now my cup...overflow.
Let new life
Here a-glow.

Source of divine energy
Stream on...stream on
Spring of vitaliy
Stream on...stream on
Spurt spiritual alacrity
Stream on...stream on

Fill the wells of salvation...roll down
From the mount.
Spout up
Through the fount.

Rivers of living water...stream on
Stream through—the mount,
Flow freely
Through the fount.

WHY

Lord why is life so complexed,
We always fail with our senseless blunders
Frequently we end up depressed?

Why does life distress
Continual pain and agony,
From such there is no rest?

Why is there so much destruction,
Man's inhumanity to man
Never seems to be any real reconstruction?

Why are there so many pills,
Just temporary relief,
Eventually they kill?

Why do problems stay,
Most see dark days,
Only few pray?

Why is there so much hate,
Apathetic feelings,
A world full of ingrates?

Why do Christians crack up,
After struggling in your service,
Drinking from life's bitter cup?

Lord why, why do we never learn
To seek you and wholly trust?
In these desperate hours
When you told us we must
Why can't we wholly trust?

THIS IS THE WAY

There is a way that seems right to man
Thinking his life consists in his wealth.
Neglecting so great a salvation
Results always in death.

Enjoying the pleasures of sin for a season
No genuine love and no spiritual tie,
Death is certainly imminent
The price is just to high.

Eat, drink, and be merry
Others to entice.
Not worried about tomorrow
Living extensively in vice.

Corrupt communication
Swearing, God is dead
Astounded, when you discover
God is still the head.

Broad is the way that leads to destruction.
Many are going in that direction today.
Please! Heed the warning sign
Stop! And consider your way.

Behold! I stand at the door and knock
If any man hear my voice,
Opens the door and accepts my grace
And makes me his choice.

I am the door
By Me if any man enter in,
I shall remove his transgressions,
And blot out all of his sins.

I came to give light
To those groping in the dark.
My Spirit is in my people
The perfect man they must mark.

I am the Good Shepherd!
I am the True Bread!
I am the True Vine!
I am the Life and Resurrection of the dead!

If you confess Jesus as Lord of your life
Eternal life is thine,
Rivers of living water will flow out of you,
Thirst no more, drink this new wine.

Yes, this is the way.
I can truly say.
Holiness everyday
Happiness all the way.

PROJECT THY TRUTH

So does my heart throb
For the wilderness heart.

So does my soul long
For the wilderness soul.

What will Thou Divine
Have me to do,
Is it to
Project Thy truth?

With your eyes
I can see.
With your heart
I will continue to weep,
For demons have conjured
Man's destiny.

Your truth
Makes us free
From the bondages
Of the thief
Who comes to
Destroy and kill,
Jesus came to destroy the works of the devil.
Doing the Father's Will.

REFLECTIONS OF TAINTED SIN

No man is an island, yet at times
Your spirit is disquieted within.
Loneliness pains your soul
Reflections of tainted sin.

Insatiable desires that can't be quenched
Overwhelmed with burning sensations.
Efficacy of prevailing situations
Subdued by various temptations.

Bound to virtual weaknesses
Indefinite quest for relief,
Escape from reason through sensuality
Summons more grief.

Hell beckons you.
Reflections of tainted sin,
The Master entreats you.
With Him new life begins.

YOUTH FOR CHRIST

In a world of vast darkness
Whose inhabitants are pervaded with vice.
Who will give the injunction—
Escape the pollution of this world
This is the challenge of youth for Christ.

In this urban society
Enveloped in malice and strife,
Who will teach the Nazarene's love
And proclaim His abundant life?

He is the Savior of all humanity
Propagating the gospel story.
Revealing the express image of God
Christ the effulgence of God's glory.

In season and out of season
Travailing diligently for souls,
Seeking the stray sheep
Bringing them into the fold.

Who will launch out into the deep
Deep into valleys of strife,
Demonstrating the Master's love?
This is the challenge of youth for Christ.

Who will preach the gospel to the poor,
Those defeated by despair?
Give them this blessed assurance
That God cares.

Who will preach the naked truth,
In spite of obstacles pray,
Asking for holy boldness
Preaching Christ is the only way?

DOES CHRIST UNDERSTAND

Most men misunderstand
Blinded by deeds underhand
Bound by the devil's brand.

They misunderstand
Struggling in sinking sand,
Denying a lifting hand.

They don't even care
About the temper flares,
About the blooming tares.

What apparent loom
What impending doom,
What hopeless gloom.

We understand
That they mis—understand,
The acceptable plan.

Thanks for the Special Man
Through eternity span,
Sent to salvage man.

Christ does understand
Desiring to impart His plan
Helping a hopeless man.

DEATH

The most unwelcomed guest
Finally arrives,
Just a usual mission
Someone to surprise.

His appearance is shocking
The company is left in sorrow,
Bid farewell
Time you cannot borrow.

He ushers you into
A chamber of eternal damnation,
Unless you had accepted
The Master's salvation.

You're young with plenty of time
Healthy with some wealth,
His shadow is near
The messenger death.

FAITH TEMPLE

Faith Temple, Faith Temple
How long have you stood,
For holiness and righteousness
And all that is good?

In the past
And now the present,
You are still
A monument.

Ministers, missionaries, souls
To you were lent,
From all walks of life
People, God sent.

Revival after revival
We use to really tarry,
Now we stand at the altar
Some of us just to marry.

We must not eat or chew gum in God's house
Is the Sunday School expression,
If we didn't take heed to anything else
That was still a good lesson.

To reverence God's house-from this training
We would not depart,
Lean not to thine own understanding.
Trust in the Lord
With all thine heart.

Faith temple, how can I forget
How you started,
With a pastor who fears God
And is softhearted.

Even though his pastorate to some
Seemed quite late,
Built on God's fundamental principle
Much faith.

Dedicated to the uplifting
Of fallen man,
Earnest intercession daily
In the midst of God's hand

GOD IS A STABILIZER

God gives stability in time of turmoil
Some consider him a strong tower.
He is the sustainer of the universe.
That is a mighty display of His power.

God helps His elect in turmoil
They don't need any transquilizers,
Not as the world giveth, but God's peace
Is a permanent stabilizer.

For the weary, He's a rock they can hold unto
For those in despair, He is a mighty fortress,
Matters not how much trouble you encounter.
God has promised and always grants rest.

Remember Job and all of his afflictions
With his insurmountable distress,
Yet God put a hedge around him
Stabilized him through the devil's test.

Just a portion of Jehovah's omnipotence
Will aid all in their persistent toil.
God always gives stability
In spite of life's devastating turmoil.

TRY IT GOD'S WAY

Live each day to the fullest
Try it God's way,
Depend on Him
From day to day.

Trust in His word
Trust in His power,
Trust in His presence
Trust in Him...every hour.

Stay on your knees in prayer
Stretch out on faith,
Be still and know Him
On God you must wait.

Don't be disturbed by delays
Oh, please pray,
His ways are not our ways
Oh, please pray

Trouble don't last always
He'll work it out someday,
Cast your cares on Him
Try it God's way.

HUNGRY AND THIRSTY

My soul is hungry and thirsty for Jehovah
My sovereign Lord,
Everyone has witnessed to this
Some even may record.

My flesh longs for God
In this dry and thirsty land,
I accept His abounding grace
I want to hold onto His unchanging hand.

The hart pants after the water brook
But my soul pants after the Lord,
God the Father, Son, and Holy Ghost
Unity, all in accord.

Jacob wrestled with the angel
A blessing he desired,
All through the night he struggled
Even though he was tired.

His name was finally changed to Israel
Which means power with God.
Like Jeremiah, I was reluctant
But now I see an almond rod.

Bless the Lord, Oh my soul
And all that is within me,
Praise Him
Salvation is free.

Now my cup is running over
His Spirit really saturates,
His love also, believe me
He freely incorporates.

Blessed are they, that hunger and thirst
For righteousness sake.
For they shall be filled, invariably
With more than they can take.

THE FATHER'S WILL

Jesus pointed us to the Father's will
Thy Kingdom come
Nevertheless, not my will...but
Thy will be done.

In earth as it is in heaven
In earth to decrease leaven,
In earth if only seven.

The Father's will can be known
And His Still small voice heard,
The Father's will can be known
Diligently reading His word.

But will we hearken
To the Father's pleading,
Or will we yield
To the Father's leading?

Father we submit our will to your will
Thy Kingdom come,
Nevertheless, not our will...but
Thy will be done.

WORLDLY SORROW

The thief comes to destroy
Steal and kill,
Every abominable act is indicative
Of His will.

Shady shackles
Bondage and yokes,
Chained captivity
With different strokes.

The troubles of life
Impairs health,
Worldly sorrow...leads
To death.

Time you cannot borrow
With worldly sorrow,
Godly sorrow is hope
For tomorrow.
Repent and be saved.

THE MASTER CARES

If you must weep mother
Just remember, God understands
Yes, you have seen many dark days
But deliverance is at hand,
You must continue on life's
Bewildering journey
Through the valley of despair.
March on diligently, mother
You are not alone—the Master cares.

Climb the highest mountain
Scale the distressing slope,
Try the loftiest summit
Oh, please climb in hope.
Mother you are weary, but don't faint now
Run with patience—endure to the end
You're paying the fare.
So many heart-aches,
So many disappointments,
So many tears,
Oh try to remember—the Master cares.

March on mother, stepping in faith
The pathway of pain must be crossed.
More suffering awaits you
But all is not lost.
Faith still maintains.
Grace eventually you will gain.

You have access to the throne
In your bosom is the phone.
When in trouble dial G-O-D.
He is the Author and Finisher
Of your faith.
When the enemy signals
With his red flare,
Oh mother, try to remember
Remember the Master cares.

Cast all of your cares upon Him
For He careth for you.
If He is aware of the sparrow's
Distant flight,
Then He is aware of your struggles
Constantly saving you from snares,
And tender traps,
Is the guiding reflecting light from above.
I believe He is a heavy load sharer.
This is the complex reality of love.
Promised to be a burden bearer
Even a friend to the bitter end.
So when you encounter much despair,
Oh mother please remember
Remember the Master cares.

SPIRITUAL EXERCISES

Lay down prostrate
Get up, up, up, on bending knees,
With hands uplifted
Lord, I wait upon Thee.

Walk by faith
And not by sight,
Serve my God
By day and by night.
Run, run, run, for Jesus
With all my might.
Stretch, stretch out on God's word.
Lean, lean, lean, over to the right.
Spirit led, walk, walk on
Gospel fed, eat, eat on,
Kept from falling
On Him I'm calling.

Lay down prostrate
Get up, up, up, on bending knees,
With hands uplifted
Lord I wait upon Thee.

Pass the test
Encourage the rest.
Mortify the flesh
Exercise unto Godliness.

WHATS THE USE

When you have tried
In spite of the suffering, scorn, abuse,
The storm becomes more severe
Oh whats the use.

I have sought the Lord
With my whole heart,
From His commandments
I did not depart.

I have shown myself a man
Walking in His ways,
Lord please help me
When I stray.

I am so frustrated
Efforts seem in vain,
If my request is granted
I need the latter rain.

I'm desolate and afflicted
These shackles have not been loosed
Preserve me in Thy love
Oh, whats the use.

DIABOLICAL MIND

Obssessed with maliciousness
Promoting strife,
Thriving on hatred
Enbittered with life.

Meditating on hell
Greed for gold,
Mammon is your god
You sold your soul.

Demon possessed
Controlled by lust,
Proud and envious
Seek help, you must.

The physician is nigh
With His healing balm,
Your soul will He ease
Your mind will He calm.

LOVE AND HATE

After a terrestrial transition
The world conceived,
Ghastly spirits of delusion
The innocent were deceived.

With a devastating explosion
The world was war torned,
All wrapped in bloody clothes
Hatred was born.

Love appeared and was tried
Innocent but yet denied,
"Save me," the thief cried
While Love was crucified.

Love is stronger than death
It prevails over hate,
Hate enslaves and destroys
Love alters your fate.

MYSTERIOUS WAYS

In the beginning was God
Creation phase,
God's purposes accomplished
Through mysterious ways.

Firmament composed
Stratospheric rays,
Spirit moved deeply
In seven days.

Darkness and darkness
Finally light was displayed,
Life appeared
Mysterious ways.

Search for the light
God says,
Salvation is born
Mysterious ways.

KINGDOM OF HEAVEN

The Kingdom of heaven
Is at hand,
On the Master's word
You can stand.

The kingdom of heaven
Is a special treasure.
Receive it now
In great measure.

Consider your ways
Cease from strife,
Embrace sound doctrine
Accept abundant life.

OVERCOME THE WORLD

In this world you'll have tribulations
The Master said,
Hated, criticized
Reviled with dread.

When you are forsaken
The Lord will take you up.
He will renew your strength always
To drink from life's bitter cup.

Your enemies against you
May lift up their heel,
God has given His precious Holy Ghost
A comforter and a seal.

Temptations will come continuously
To do you severe harm,
Submit yourself to God
Resist the devil's charm.

Conformed not to this world
Stop walking with the crowd,
Stand up for Jesus
Start crying aloud!

People think they do God's service
By harming you,
Lo, He's with you always
Don't be so blue.

Overcome the world
Jesus Christ did,
He's manifested to you,
From the world He's hid.

PRAY FOR ME

Atossa, from frequent observation
I've noticed many a thing,
You're a friend of God
With great joy you always sing.

You're dedicated to one end
To please your Lord.
Strong in the faith
With Him in accord.

You have excelled in God's Spirit
You're really anointed,
In God's providence
You're divinely appointed.

You have an excellent spirit
You're a true missionary,
God's revelation and inspiration
You always carry.

A ministry of prayer
God has given you,
Power with Him
Miracles granted too.

Atossa—I have a request
I know you will not rest,
Until you do your best
Even though it seems hopeless.

Oh-ask-Him, ask the Master
Ask a blessing for me,
I need Him—tell Him, I need Him.
Oh tell Him please.

I want to be clothed with humility
I want to be meek,
I've tried so very hard to run
With my vision.
Sometimes I am just to weak.

PRAYER OF FAITH

With the power, authority, and the ability
Of the almighty God.
Curseth be this affliction that's common
It's not odd.

In the name of Jesus
Lord do it today,
Let your healing virtue flow
In this impotent body I pray.

From the crown of the head
To the sole of the feet,
Lord grant and restore
Health complete.

With the perpetual faith
Of the Son of God,
For everyone I pray
Even Todd.

God deliver
God make whole,
Liberate from this infirmity
Refine this soul.

Woman accept your healing
Man your deliverance.
Everybody, praise God, sing
Shout and dance.

FATHER HOW LONG

How long will Thou forget me
Oh Lord, forever?
I need divine guidance
The wicked one is so clever.

How long will Thou hide Thy face from me
While I water my bed with my tears?
Hast Thou withdrawn Thine hand from me
After such intimate years?

How long shall I go on mourning
With sorrow in my heart?
While prevailing circumstances
Rend it apart.

Hear me and take into consideration
This petition that is so desperate,
Allay this pulsating pain
And boost my little faith.

Lest the enemy prevails against me
And I sleep the sleep of death.
Man's extremity, Oh Lord, is your opportunity
Revive me and prosper my health.

Because I have trusted in your mercy
Father, your grace will sustain me.
My heart shall rejoice in your salvation.
My hope is resting in Thee

I will sing unto Jehovah-Rapha
He healed my broken heart,
He laid His hands upon me
And removed this terrible scar.

Yes there is a balm in Gilead.
Whose worth cannot be appraised,
Yes there is a physician there.
Who is worthy of my praise.

He is help for the hopeless
Are you heavy laden and desire rest?
He is hope for the helpless
You He wants to bless.

Try Him now, don't wait
Please! Don't procrastinate.
There is nothing too hard for the Lord
Seek Him right away
In holiness partake.

TURN US AGAIN

Lord, how long will You feed us
With the bread of tears,
When will your wrath pass over
And quiet our fears.

In great measure Thou givest us
Tears to drink,
Our relationship has become
A broken link.

We have gone out of the way
We have gone astray.
We are dying on broadway
We're going back to the narrow way
It's not too late.
We'll humble ourselves
And pray.

Oh Lord, God of hosts
Turn us again, turn us around
Save us...plant our feet
On higher ground.

He is the Author and Finisher
Of our faith.
Wonderful Counselor
He is great.

Greater than
The most powerful man.
Greater than,
The most evil hand.

Greater than
Technological power,
Greater than
The tallest
Tower.

Greater than
The devil's schemes
Greater is
The Supreme.

He is greater than
Your imagination.
His greatness increases
Your anticipation.

Greater is He that is in you
Than He that is in the world.
Great is His faithfulness
Accept this valuable pearl.

REVIVE ME

Oh Lord, ever before me
Is my sin.
Genetically imputed
From within.

I acknowledge my iniquity
Cleanse me from my impurity.

I have only
Sinned against Thee
I am lonely
Have mercy upon me.

Oh Lord revive me
My spirit renew,
Wash me with hyysop
Purge me too.

A clean heart
In me create
My transgressing ways
Oh please abate.

Now salvation joy
Restore unto me,
Now salvation peace
Grant it please.

Lord revive me
Refurbish my spirit, revive my soul
Lord revive me.
Revive me, revive me in the fold.

Deliver me from bloodguiltiness.
Lord forgive my foolishness.
I offer you my spirit rended apart
I offer you my broken heart.

Lord revive me, in my soul
Let the joy bells ring.
In my heart
Give me a new song to sing.

FORTHCOMING BOOKS BY ALPHONSO CRAWFORD:

CROSSROADS: POEMS ON RACE/POLITICS/LIFE

TWO HEARTS:LOVE POEMS/LOVE LETTERS

100 WAYS FOR PEOPLE TO GET HEALED

100 SYMBOLS OF HEALTH AND HEALING

THE THREE GREATEST CHALLENGES OF LIFE

ADVANCED HEALING MANUAL

HEALTH AND HEALING WORKBOOK

LEADERSHIP IN AN AGE OF CRISIS: 25 OBSERVATIONS

LEADERSHIP: 25 PITFALLS/POWER TOOLS

LEADERSHIP: 25 FACTS ABOUT LEADERS

LEADERSHIP: TOUGH QUESTIONS/TOUGH ANSWERS

POWER: 25 FACTS ABOUT POWER

POWERS THAT WOMEN HAVE

WISDOM: 25 FACTS ABOUT WISDOM

WISDOM PERSPECTIVES: 25 INSIGHTS

TRIUMPHANT: 25 WAYS TO EXCEL IN LIFE

DOMINATE: 25 DOMINION PRINCIPLES

WHY GOD MADE BLACK PEOPLE BLACK:
25 REASONS WHY

DREAMS: 25 FEATURES OF A DREAM

GOD'S WILL: 25 WAYS TO KNOW GOD'S WILL FOR YOUR LIFE

ADVANCED INTERPERSONAL COMMUNICATION: 25 EXPRESSIONS

THE POWER OF BIG THINKING: 25 LAWS

SPIRITUOTHERAPY: 25 PRINCIPLES

MEN: 25 FACTS ABOUT MEN

PERSONALITY PROFILES

FORTHCOMING BOOKS BY ELEANOR CRAWFORD:

WOMEN IN MINISTRY: 25 WAYS TO IMPACT THE WORLD

WOMEN: 25 FACTS ABOUT WOMEN

WOMEN: 25 WOMEN THAT CHANGED HISTORY

WOMEN OF DESTINY: 25 CHALLENGES

WOMEN'S MANUAL: 25 LIFE LESSONS

WOMEN OF WISDOM: 25 INSIGHTS

WOMEN'S RESOURCES: 25 ASSETS

WOMEN'S WORKBOOKS: 25 ACTIVITIES

WOMEN'S SERMONS: 25 SERMONS

WOMEN AND MEN: 25 CONTRASTS

WOMEN'S QUIZ BOOK

WOMEN'S DEVOTIONAL BOOK

WOMEN'S AFFIRMATION BOOK

FORTHCOMING BOOKS BY BYRON CRAWFORD:

SELL YOUR WAY TO SUCCESS: 25 WAYS TO SUCCEED IN LIFE

SUCCESS IN LIFE: 25 STEPS TO THE TOP

LAWS OF SUCCESS: 25 LAWS

SUCCESS SECRETS: 25 INSIGHTS

SYNONYMS FOR SUCCESS: 25 CORRELATIONS

SUCCESS MANUAL: 25 LIFE LESSONS

SUCCESS WORKBOOK: 25 ACTIVITIES

SUCCESSFUL STRATEGIC PLANNING: 25 TACTICS

SUCCESS QUIZ BOOK

SUCCESS DEVOTIONAL BOOK

SUCCESS AFFIRMATION BOOK

SUCCESS SERMONS: 25 SUCCESS SERMONS

SIGN UP AND BE NOTIFIED FOR SEMINARS/WORKSHOPS/CONFERENCES

NAME_____

ADDRESS_____

CITY_____

STATE_____ZIP CODE_____

PHONE NO._____

EMAIL ADDRESS_____

SEND TO:

NEW LIFE EDUCATIONAL SERVICES
P.O. BOX 96
OAK LAWN, ILLINOIS 60454

SEMINARS/WORKSHOPS/CONFERENCES

- ANNUAL WOMEN'S LUNCHEON
- ANNUAL MEN'S LUNCHEON
- HEALTH AND HEALING
- LEADERSHIP DEVELOPMENT
- DREAMS AND VISION
- PERSONAL POWER
- GIFTS AND TALENTS
- RELATIONSHIPS
- PROBLEM SOLVING
- FIVEFOLD MINISTRY
- INTERPRETING THE TIMES
- GOD'S WILL FOR YOUR LIFE
- STRATEGIC PLANNING
- ADVANCED INTERPERSONAL COMMUNICATION
- THE DYNAMICS OF PURPOSE
- NEGOTIATION SKILLS
- HOW TO SELL YOURSELF
- TEAM BUILDING
- MANAGING SELF
- MANAGING CONFLICT
- MANAGING STRESS
- SELF MOTIVATION
- PEOPLE MOTIVATION
- HOW TO COUNSEL
- SUCCESS STRATEGIES
- HOW TO START A BUSINESS
- HOW TO START A SCHOOL
- HOW TO HOME SHOOL
- NEEDS OF WOMEN AND MEN
- NEEDS OF CHILDREN
- TIME MANAGEMENT
- SOCIAL SKILLS
- BIG THINKING POWER

- SELF DECEPTION: HOW WE LIE TO OURSELVES EVERYDAY
- LIFELONG LEARNING
- FEEDBACK
- LAWS OF LIFE
- VISION
- SETTING GOALS
- CHANGE AGENTS
- BECOMING A CONSULTANT
- MOTIVATIONAL SPEAKING
- 100 YARD DASH VERSUS THE 20,000 METER RACE
- WEALTH IN YOU
- MARRIAGE RENEWAL
- CREATING JOBS
- LAWS OF LIFE
- HOW TO GUARD YOUR HEART
- MENTORING

ABOUT THE AUTHOR

Dr. Alphonso Crawford is an apostle of health and healing. Dr. Crawford is the president of New Life Educational Services. He pastors Cathedral Of Prayer with his wife.

Dr. Crawford received his background in biblical studies from Moody Bible Institute.

He has a B.A. from DePaul University, the Master Of Divinity from McCormick Theological Seminary, the Doctor Of Ministry from Chicago Theological Seminary. respectively at the University Of Chicago.

www.ingramcontent.com/pod-product-compliance
Lightning Source LLC
Chambersburg PA
CBHW072037060426
42449CB00010BA/2314